just

SAUCES.

just

A LITTLE BOOK OF FINISHING TOUCHES

SAUCES.

The Editors of Lyons Press

Lyons Press
Guilford, Connecticut

An imprint of Globe Pequot Press

Copyright © 2011 by Morris Book Publishing, LLC

Lyons Press is an imprint of Globe Pequot Press.

Library of Congress Cataloging-in-Publication Data is available on file.

ISBN 978-1-59921-941-7

The information in this book is true and complete to the best of our knowledge. All recommendations are made without guarantee on the part of Globe Pequot Press. Globe Pequot Press disclaims any liability in connection with the use of this information.

Printed in China

10 9 8 7 6 5 4 3 2 1

CONTENTS

Creamy, salty, tangy, sweet . . . sauces tempt even the pickiest of taste buds.

Sauces, in all their infinite wisdom, can make or break a meal. And when they break a meal—well, you will have a mess on your hands. A good sauce can mask the mistakes of overcooked chicken and tough meat, but very rarely can anything mask an overcooked sauce. Sauces have even been lauded for their undeniable ability to trick children—and adults, too—into eating vegetables. Nothing makes asparagus more appetizing than a mayo dipping sauce.

Sauce comes from the French language, derived from the Latin word *salsus*, meaning salted. For the purposes of this book, we have included traditional tomato and cream sauces along with the likes of fruity chutneys, tangy marinades, zesty salsas, sweet glazes, and dipping sauces.

A good sauce isn't difficult to make, but it often takes patience and practice. So whether you are looking for a quick sauce to pour over pasta, a spicy dipping sauce to accompany an appetizer, or a delicious marinade to prepare chicken, *Just Sauces* will have *just* the recipe for you ●

TYPES OF SAUCES

CHUTNEY

Chutneys can be classified in two basic categories: fresh chutneys, those that are blended with fresh ingredients and spices and require no cooking; and cooked chutneys, those simmered over a low heat till the flavors are blended.

CREAM SAUCE

Also known as a white sauce or Alfredo sauce, a cream sauce is made by cooking flour in fat, then adding broth and milk or cream. The most common cream sauce dish is fettuccini Alfredo.

DIPPING SAUCE

Dipping sauces, popular in Asian cuisine, are served as a condiment alongside finger foods, grilled fish or meat, seafood, and vegetables. Flavor combinations for dipping sauces are limitless.

GLAZE

A glaze can be made from a sauce that has been reduced to a syrupy consistency. It can also be

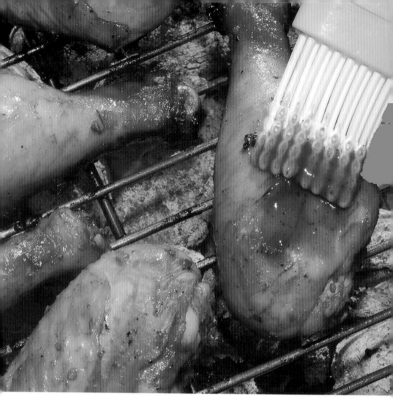

made from a liquid mixture, thickened or not, that is brushed onto meat, fish, or poultry that is then grilled or broiled. A glaze is usually shiny and highly flavored. It can be used on all types of meat, fish and poultry. Glazes usually have some sweet ingredients so they will brown, thicken, and turn shiny in the heat.

GRAVY

Gravy, that bane of Thanksgiving hosts, can be made several ways. You can just add a slurry of flour and water to the drippings remaining in the pan and stir vigorously with a whisk. Or make a roux with fat and flour, then add broth made from the giblets and turkey neck. The secret to the best gravy is adding enough salt. Keep adding salt and tasting. When the flavor blooms, you've added enough.

MARINADE

Marinades are used to flavor meats, poultry, vegetables, and seafood before cooking. For best results, foods should be soaked in marinades for hours or overnight in the refrigerator. Be sure to discard any unused marinade to prevent contamination from raw food.

REDUCTION

The point of reduction is to concentrate and increase flavor, so you have to start with high-quality ingredients. Use homemade or boxed stocks, and don't be afraid of herbs and spices. When reducing a sauce,

watch it carefully. It can go from burnished and perfect to burnt in seconds. You can reduce sauces right in the pan over high heat, or reduce liquid, then add to the pan to create a sauce.

TOMATO SAUCE

The most common of sauces, tomato sauce is usually served over cooked pasta. Since tomatoes are easily grown in many climates, they are readily available in most areas. Look for tomatoes that are brightly colored and heavy for their size. Hothouse tomatoes and tomatoes with some of the vine still attached are usually more flavorful. Large, juicy tomatoes make good candidates for a delicious sauce.

SALSA

Fresh tomatoes are often chopped up with onions, garlic, and cilantro to make a condiment known as salsa. They are also pureed with other ingredients such as fresh green chiles, jalapeños, onions, or garlic to create different types of salsa. The fresher and riper the tomatoes are, the better your salsa will taste, so be sure to use the best tomatoes you can find.

SIMPLE PAN SAUCE

A pan sauce uses the browned bits left behind in a pan after the cooking of meat or poultry. The secrets to a simple pan sauce are to brown meat thoroughly, use a flavorful liquid, and season it well. Chicken broth or stock is one of the best liquids for making a pan sauce, but you can use marinades or liquids from vegetables or fruits. For a nice finish for a simple pan sauce, swirl in a tablespoon of butter at the last second. Taste the sauce before serving and add more salt or pepper if necessary ●

Glazed Chicken Wings

INGREDIENTS

24 chicken wings
1 cup soy sauce, divided
³/₄ cup rice wine
¹/₄ cup rice wine vinegar
1 tablespoon sugar
1 onion or 2 green onions, chopped
1 tablespoon chopped ginger root
3 cloves garlic, chopped

Vegetable oil for frying
2 tablespoons honey
1 teaspoon hot chile oil
2 tablespoons sesame seeds

YIELD: 6 SERVINGS

1. Separate chicken wings into three pieces at the joints; discard the tips. In a bowl, whisk together $3/4$ cup soy sauce, wine, vinegar, and sugar.

2. Place chopped onion, ginger root, and garlic in a large resealable plastic bag. Pour sauce mixture in the bag and add chicken wings; refrigerate 8 hours or overnight. Turn bag occasionally.

3. Fry wings in hot oil until golden brown, about 4-5 minutes. Drain on paper towels.

4. In a small bowl, whisk together remaining soy sauce, honey, and hot chile oil.

5. Brush honey–soy sauce over cooked chicken wings. Sprinkle with sesame seeds.

For extra heat, add more chile oil to the glaze, or serve the wings with a side of chile paste along with hoisin sauce.

Orange-Glazed Chicken Salad

INGREDIENTS

$1/2$ cup orange marmalade
2 tablespoons light soy sauce
Juice of $1/2$ orange, freshly squeezed
1 teaspoon freshly grated ginger root
$1/2$ teaspoon red pepper flakes, or to taste
1 pound boneless, skinless chicken breasts or thighs
2 cups arugula or other greens
$1/2$ cup citrus dressing or vinaigrette
1 cup cooked wild or brown rice (optional)
Optional garnishes: dried cranberries; toasted pine nuts; water chestnuts, drained and rinsed; mandarin oranges, drained and rinsed

YIELD: 4 SERVINGS

1. Preheat broiler to 350°F; set rack 8–10 inches from heat source. Mix first five ingredients together in a small bowl; warm in microwave for 90 seconds or until marmalade is melted.

2. Place chicken on pan sprayed with nonstick cooking spray; coat with orange glaze. Broil 5 minutes per side, being careful not to burn. Turn; brush glaze on second side and broil another 5 minutes.

3. Cut chicken into strips; arrange greens on platter. Pour dressing over greens. Mix rice with chicken. Spoon chicken over greens; garnish as desired.

Sweet and Hot Glazed Meatballs

INGREDIENTS

2 tablespoons butter
1 onion, chopped
3 cloves garlic, minced
1 cup beef broth, divided
$\frac{1}{2}$ cup apple jelly
1 star anise
1 pinch ground cloves
$\frac{1}{3}$ cup brown mustard
$\frac{1}{4}$ cup brown sugar
$\frac{1}{4}$ cup apple cider vinegar
$\frac{1}{8}$ teaspoon cayenne pepper
$\frac{1}{2}$ teaspoon hot pepper sauce
50 small frozen fully cooked meatballs, thawed
1 tablespoon cornstarch

YIELD: 8–10 SERVINGS

1. In small saucepan, heat butter and cook onion and garlic over medium heat for 5–6 minutes.

2. Add $\frac{3}{4}$ cup broth and bring to a simmer; add apple jelly and stir to melt. Pour into 4- or 5-quart slow cooker.

3. Add star anise, cloves, mustard, sugar, vinegar, pepper, and pepper sauce; stir; add meatballs. Cover; cook on low 7-9 hours.

4. Remove star anise. In small bowl, mix cornstarch with rest of broth; add to slow cooker. Cover and cook on high until sauce thickens.

Other varieties of jelly would work well in this recipe. Try pineapple jelly, apricot preserves, or raspberry jelly for a new flavor.

Asian Glazed Ribs

INGREDIENTS

2 (2-pound) racks baby back ribs
½ teaspoon salt
¼ teaspoon pepper
1 teaspoon five-spice powder
2 tablespoons olive oil
2 onions, chopped
1 cup barbecue sauce
¼ cup hoisin sauce
3 tablespoons honey
3 tablespoons soy sauce
2 tablespoons Dijon mustard
3 cloves garlic, minced
1 tablespoon minced ginger root

YIELD: 6 SERVINGS

1. Preheat oven to 375°F. Cut ribs into two-rib portions and place in roasting pan. Sprinkle with salt, pepper, and five-spice powder; drizzle with olive oil.

2. Roast ribs for 1 hour; remove and drain. Place onions in 4- or 5-quart slow cooker; top with ribs.

3. Combine remaining ingredients in bowl and pour over ribs.

4. Cover and cook on low for 8–9 hours, or on high for 4–5 hours, until ribs are very tender.

Glazed Spareribs

2-pound rack of pork spareribs, tops trimmed
3 tablespoons soy sauce, divided
1 tablespoon hoisin sauce
1 teaspoon sesame oil
$\frac{1}{4}$ teaspoon five-spice powder (optional)
$\frac{1}{4}$ teaspoon salt
$\frac{1}{4}$ teaspoon pepper
1 teaspoon brown sugar
1 teaspoon rice wine vinegar
1 clove garlic, pressed
2 tablespoons honey
$\frac{1}{2}$ cup hot water

YIELD: 6 SERVINGS

1. Cut rack into two-rib sections. Line a baking dish with nonstick foil.

2. Combine 2 tablespoons soy sauce, hoisin sauce, sesame oil, five-spice powder (if using), salt, pepper, brown sugar, and rice vinegar.

3. Brush ribs with sauce. Place ribs on baking dish. Cover and refrigerate 6–8 hours. Remove and let stand 15 minutes.

GLAZES

4. Roast ribs in 350°F oven 50 minutes, turning occasionally. Combine 1 tablespoon soy sauce and remaining ingredients; baste ribs and roast 10 minutes longer.

Glazed Root Vegetables

INGREDIENTS

1 onion, chopped
3 cloves garlic, minced
3 carrots, cut into chunks
1 parsnip, peeled and cubed
1 turnip, peeled and cubed
2 sweet potatoes, peeled and cubed
3 russet potatoes, peeled and cubed
$\frac{1}{2}$ cup water
1 teaspoon salt
$\frac{1}{8}$ teaspoon pepper
$\frac{1}{4}$ cup honey
2 tablespoons brown sugar
2 tablespoons butter
1 tablespoon cornstarch

YIELD: 6–8 SERVINGS

1. Combine onion, garlic, carrots, parsnip, turnip, sweet potatoes, and russet potatoes in 4- or 5-quart slow cooker.

2. Add water, salt, and pepper and stir. Cover and cook on low for 7–9 hours or until vegetables are tender.

3. In bowl, combine honey, brown sugar, butter, and cornstarch and mix well. Pour into slow cooker.

4. Cover and cook on high for 45–60 minutes or until vegetables are glazed and tender.

You can flavor the glaze any way you'd like. Use the basic ingredients: honey, butter, and cornstarch. Then add heat with jalapeño or habañero peppers, or with chile powder or ground chiles. Double the glaze for a holiday casserole, or flavor it with cinnamon, allspice, nutmeg, and cardamom. You can make the glaze ahead of time; cover it and store in the refrigerator. Make sure you stir before adding to the food.

Pineapple-Glazed Ham Half

INGREDIENTS

1 (5–6-pound) half ham, fully cooked
2 cups apple wood chips, soaked
1 cup pineapple juice
2 tablespoons butter
3 tablespoons Dijon mustard

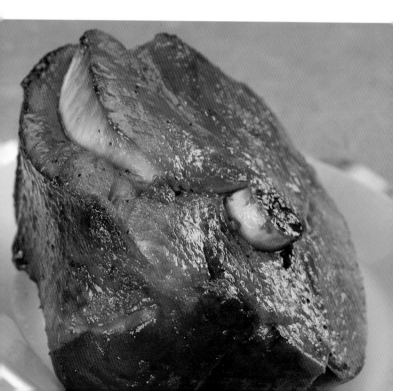

2 tablespoons honey

$\frac{1}{4}$ teaspoon pepper

$\frac{1}{2}$ cup brown sugar

YIELD: 8-10 SERVINGS

1. Place ham on grill over indirect low heat. Place soaked wood chips in drip pan. Cover; grill for 10 minutes.

2. Meanwhile, combine juice, butter, mustard, honey, pepper in small saucepan and bring to a simmer.

3. Turn and brush the ham with juice mixture every 20 minutes. Keep grilling until the ham registers 150°F in two different places, about 1 hour.

4. Sprinkle ham with brown sugar. Grill ham; turn frequently and continue sprinkling with sugar, until ham is glazed, 15-20 minutes.

Leftover ham is one of the best parts of the holidays. Use your grilled ham in sandwiches, soups, and salads.

Glazed Pork Tenderloin

INGREDIENTS

1 tablespoon olive oil
3 cloves garlic, minced
$\frac{1}{2}$ cup minced onion
1 star anise
1 tablespoon brown sugar
2 tablespoons rice wine vinegar
1 tablespoon chile paste
1 tablespoon grated ginger root
$\frac{1}{2}$ teaspoon ground ginger
$\frac{1}{2}$ teaspoon pepper
1 tablespoon low-sodium soy sauce
2 (1$\frac{1}{2}$-pound) pork tenderloins

YIELD: 8 SERVINGS

1. In large heavy-duty plastic bag, combine all ingredients except tenderloins.

2. Pierce tenderloins with fork 10 times each. Add to bag with other ingredients. Seal and knead.

3. Place in glass dish; marinate in refrigerator 8–24 hours. Preheat oven to 400°F.

4. Place tenderloins and marinade in glass dish; remove star anise. Bake 35 to 45 minutes, until meat thermometer registers 150°F. Cover, let stand 5 minutes, then serve.

Glazed Fish Fillets

INGREDIENTS

1 tablespoon olive oil
4 cloves garlic, minced
$1/4$ cup minced onion
3 tablespoons balsamic vinegar
$1/2$ teaspoon dry mustard

2 tablespoons honey
1 teaspoon dried tarragon
$\frac{1}{8}$ teaspoon pepper
6 (6-ounce) red snapper fillets

YIELD: 6 SERVINGS

1. In small saucepan heat olive oil over medium heat. Add garlic and onion; cook and stir 5–6 minutes, until light golden brown.

2. Add vinegar, mustard, honey, tarragon, and pepper; cook and stir until sauce blends.

3. Prepare and preheat grill. Place a sheet of heavy-duty foil on the grill; pierce it several times with a knife.

4. Place fish on foil that has been sprayed with nonstick cooking spray; brush with sauce. Cover and grill 5 minutes per inch of thickness, brushing with sauce, until fish flakes. Discard sauce.

Balsamic vinegar is an aged vinegar that has a sweet taste, dark color, and slightly thickened texture. It is expensive, but a bottle lasts a long time and its flavor is incomparable.

Salmon with Orange Sauce

INGREDIENTS

1 tablespoon unsalted butter
3 cloves garlic, minced
2 tablespoons grated ginger root
$\frac{3}{4}$ cup orange juice
1 teaspoon orange zest
1 teaspoon dried tarragon
$\frac{1}{8}$ teaspoon pepper
1 teaspoon reduced-sodium soy sauce
4 (6-ounce) salmon fillets
1 tablespoon cornstarch
1 tablespoon lemon juice
$\frac{1}{4}$ cup white wine

YIELD: 4 SERVINGS

1. In small saucepan heat butter; add garlic and ginger. Cook and stir 4–5 minutes, until tender.

2. Add orange juice, zest, tarragon, pepper, and soy sauce; simmer 2 minutes.

3. Place salmon on broiler rack; brush with some of the orange mixture. Broil under preheated broiler 4 minutes.

4. Carefully turn salmon, brush with sauce, and continue broiling. Add cornstarch, lemon

juice, and wine to orange sauce; simmer
while fish cooks 3–5 minutes longer. Serve
with fish.

You can make this recipe using grapefruit
juice or lemon juice in place of the orange
juice, or use a combination of citrus juices
and zest.

Filet Mignon with Caramel Glaze

INGREDIENTS

2 tablespoons butter
3 cloves garlic, minced
2 tablespoons brown sugar
1 tablespoon honey
$\frac{1}{3}$ cup balsamic vinegar
$\frac{1}{3}$ cup beef stock
1 teaspoon salt, divided
$\frac{1}{4}$ teaspoon pepper, divided
4 (6-ounce) filet mignon steaks
2 tablespoons olive oil

YIELD: 4 STEAKS

1. Cook and stir garlic in butter for 3 minutes. Add brown sugar and honey; cook and stir until mixture combines.

2. Add vinegar, stock, half of the salt, and pepper and bring to a simmer. Reduce heat to low and simmer for 10–15 minutes or until syrupy. Remove from heat.

3. Let steaks stand at room temperature for 30 minutes, then pat dry. Sprinkle with remaining salt and pepper and brush with olive oil.

4. Grill steaks over direct heat for 8–11 minutes, turning twice, to desired doneness. Plate and top with sauce.

The filet mignon and tenderloin come from a part of the cow that isn't weight-bearing and isn't involved in movement, so the meat is very tender. The back rib cage is the source for these cuts as well as prime rib. The texture is very soft and tender, with a mild beefy flavor.

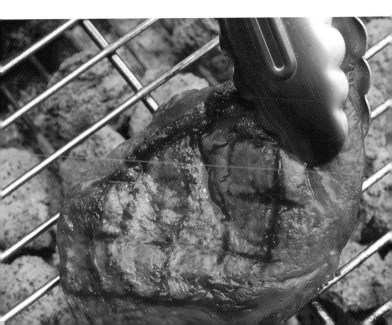

Apricot-Glazed
Chicken Breasts

INGREDIENTS

3 cups water
1 cup apricot nectar
⅓ cup salt
⅓ cup sugar
1 cup apple cider vinegar

6-8 boneless, skinless chicken breasts
1/2 cup apricot preserves
1 tablespoon lemon juice
1 tablespoon honey
1 teaspoon vanilla
1 teaspoon ground ginger
3 tablespoons Dijon mustard

YIELD: 6 SERVINGS

1. Combine water, nectar, salt, sugar, and vinegar; mix well. Pound chicken until 1/2 inch thick; add to brine; cover; refrigerate for 3-4 hours.

2. Combine remaining ingredients and refrigerate.

3. Preheat grill. Drain chicken. Place over direct medium-high heat. Brush with half of the preserves mixture.

4. After 3 minutes, turn chicken and brush with remaining glaze. Grill for 3-4 minutes or until chicken is almost cooked. Turn once more; cook for 30-45 seconds until temperature reaches 160°F. Let stand; serve.

For a sauce to accompany the chicken, just double the glaze. Boil it for 2 minutes before serving with the chicken.

Marinated Pork Souvlaki

INGREDIENTS

1 lemon
3 tablespoons olive oil
2 tablespoons balsamic vinegar
2 tablespoons red wine
1 teaspoon dill weed
1/4 teaspoon dried mint leaves
1/4 teaspoon pepper
1 tablespoon fresh oregano
2 pounds pork tenderloin
2 red onions
3 green bell peppers

YIELD: 8 SERVINGS

1. Prepare grill. Juice lemon; remove zest. Combine juice, zest, olive oil, vinegar, wine, dill, mint, pepper, and oregano in a bowl.

2. Cut pork into 1½-inch cubes and add to marinade. Cover and chill 8–24 hours.

3. Remove pork from marinade; reserve marinade. Cut each onion into eight wedges; cut bell peppers into strips. Thread food onto skewers.

4. Grill 6 inches from medium coals 12–15 minutes. Brush with marinade until pork registers 155°F. Discard remaining marinade. Serve with tzatziki sauce, made from half a peeled and seeded cucumber, 1 cup sour cream, 2 tablespoons lemon juice, 2 minced cloves garlic, 1 tablespoon fresh dill, and ¼ teaspoon pepper.

This marinade recipe is quite variable and forgiving. You can use lime juice instead, add garlic, or omit the mint. Use other fresh herbs, omit the balsamic vinegar, and add hot minced chile peppers. You can make the marinade ahead of time. Store it in the refrigerator for up to 2 days. If you change the marinade and love the results, be sure to write down your formula. Soon, you'll have a notebook full of tried-and-true recipes.

Honey-Mustard Pork Tenderloin

INGREDIENTS

2 tablespoons low-sodium soy sauce
2 tablespoons olive oil
2 garlic cloves, minced
2 tablespoons honey
3 tablespoons Dijon mustard
$\frac{1}{2}$ teaspoon ground ginger
$\frac{1}{4}$ teaspoon pepper
2 (1-pound) pork tenderloins

YIELD: 3–4 SERVINGS

1. Combine soy sauce, oil, garlic, honey, mustard, ginger, and pepper. Add tenderloins; cover and chill for 8–12 hours.

2. Drain tenderloins, reserving marinade. Pat tenderloins dry with paper towel.

3. Grill tenderloins over direct medium heat for 3 minutes, then turn $\frac{1}{4}$ turn and cook for 3 minutes longer.

4. Move tenderloins over drip pan, turn $\frac{1}{4}$ turn, and grill, covered, for 7–10 minutes longer, turning and brushing with reserved marinade until temperature registers 150°F. Remove from the grill, cover, and let rest for 10 minutes.

Marinated Lamb Chops

INGREDIENTS

1 cup yogurt, beaten
1 teaspoon cumin powder
1 teaspoon coriander powder
½ teaspoon black pepper

$^1/_2$ teaspoon red chile powder

1 teaspoon garam masala powder

$^1/_2$ teaspoon salt

2 tablespoons vegetable oil

2 tablespoons fresh lemon juice

8 lamb rib chops, trimmed of extra fat

YIELD: 3-4 SERVINGS

1. Combine all the ingredients except the lamb in a large shallow bowl.

2. Add the lamb and stir to coat well. Cover and marinate in the refrigerator for at least 3 hours or overnight.

3. Place the lamb on a greased baking sheet, discarding any excess marinade. Bake in a preheated 425°F oven 25–20 minutes until meat is tender and cooked through.

Yogurt is commonly used for marinating meats in Indian cooking. Marinating the lamb chops in yogurt will help tenderize the meat and impart a delightful flavor.

Lamb Ribs with Lemon Herb Marinade

INGREDIENTS

3$\frac{1}{2}$ pounds lamb ribs, Frenched
3 tablespoons olive oil
1 onion, minced
3 cloves garlic, minced
$\frac{1}{3}$ cup lemon juice
2 tablespoons brown sugar
1 teaspoon salt
$\frac{1}{4}$ teaspoon white pepper
1 teaspoon lemon zest
2 tablespoons finely chopped mint
2 tablespoons chopped flat-leaf parsley
1 tablespoon fresh thyme leaves

YIELD: 6 SERVINGS

1. Place ribs in large casserole. Combine remaining ingredients in small bowl; pour over lamb.

2. Cover lamb; refrigerate for 8–12 hours. Remove from marinade, reserving marinade.

3. Prepare grill for indirect heat. Rub grate with oil, and add lamb ribs, meat side down, over medium indirect heat.

MARINADES

4. Grill for 7 minutes, then turn and brush with remaining marinade. Cover; grill for 6 minutes longer. Finish by searing lamb over direct heat for 3 minutes on each side. Let stand 10 minutes.

Spatchcocked Chicken with Garlic Marinade

INGREDIENTS

6 cloves garlic, minced
2 teaspoons salt
$1/2$ teaspoon pepper
$1/2$ teaspoon garlic powder
2 teaspoons paprika
$1/4$ cup olive oil
2 tablespoons butter
1 (3–4-pound) whole chicken

YIELD: 4-6 SERVINGS

1. Mix garlic with salt, pepper, garlic powder, and paprika, oil, and butter.

2. With kitchen shears or sharp knife, cut the backbone out of the chicken. Place chicken, bone side down, on work surface. Press down on the chicken breast to flatten chicken.

3. Loosen skin and rub on half of the garlic mixture. Smooth skin over flesh and rub in remaining mixture.

4. Refrigerate for 8-12 hours. Grill chicken, skin side down, on direct medium heat for 15 minutes. Turn; grill for 20–25 minutes longer until 170°F.

Spatchcock sounds like such a fancy English term. It actually originated in Ireland. All it means is a chicken with its backbone removed so it will lay flat on the grill; it's a butterflied chicken.

Marinated Grilled Shrimp

INGREDIENTS

1/4 cup olive oil
4 cloves garlic, minced
1/4 cup minced red onion
1 (14-ounce) can diced tomatoes, drained
1/3 cup seafood cocktail sauce
2 tablespoons lemon juice
2 teaspoons chopped fresh oregano leaves
1/8 teaspoon black pepper
1/8 teaspoon cayenne pepper
3 pounds peeled large shrimp

YIELD: 8 SERVINGS

1. Cook garlic and onion in olive oil until tender, 4 minutes.

2. Pour into food processor; cool for 15 minutes. Add drained tomatoes, sauce, lemon juice, oregano, and peppers; blend.

3. Pour into large bowl; add shrimp. Cover; chill for 1 hour. Drain shrimp, reserving marinade. Double-skewer shrimp, pushing them close together.

4. Grill shrimp over direct medium heat, brushing with marinade, for 5–6 minutes, turning once, until shrimp curl and turn pink. Boil marinade to serve with shrimp.

Orange-Marinated Sesame Sea Bass

INGREDIENTS

6 1-inch-thick sea bass fillets
3 tablespoons soy sauce
1 cup orange juice
Juice of 1 lemon
$\frac{1}{2}$ teaspoon sugar
2 tablespoons dark sesame oil
1 tablespoon grated ginger root
1 tablespoon rice wine
$\frac{1}{4}$ teaspoon hot chile oil
1 orange, quartered
1 tablespoon sesame seeds

YIELD: 6 SERVINGS

1. Rinse bass fillets and pat dry; place in a baking dish.

2. Whisk together soy sauce, orange juice, lemon juice, sugar, sesame oil, ginger root, wine, and chile oil.

3. Pour marinade over fillets, cover, and refrigerate 1 hour.

4. Remove fillets from the marinade; place in a steamer basket. Place quartered orange in

wok and add water to a level just below the fish. Cover the steamer.

5. Bring the water to a boil; reduce heat to medium. Steam fish 8–10 minutes, until fillets are opaque.

6. Boil marinade until reduced by half. Drizzle over fillets, garnish with sesame seeds, and serve.

Mango and Mint Chutney

INGREDIENTS

1 large ripe mango, peeled and chopped
8-10 fresh mint leaves
1 tablespoon sugar
2 tablespoons fresh lemon juice
Pinch of salt

YIELD: 3-4 SERVINGS

1. Blend all the ingredients together in a food processor or blender until smooth.

2. Serve cold.

Mangoes are one of the most popular fruits in India, and it is no surprise that Indian cuisine makes use of them in very creative ways. This recipe is a great accompaniment to most deep-fried finger foods, as well as making a nice addition to a spicy curry meal. You can use any kind of mangoes that are in season—just make sure they are well ripened to get an intense sweet flavor.

Cilantro Chutney

INGREDIENTS

2 cups chopped fresh cilantro
8-10 fresh mint leaves
1 green chile, roughly chopped
1 cup plain yogurt, beaten
2 tablespoons fresh lemon juice
1/4 teaspoon cumin powder
Salt, to taste

YIELD: 3-4 SERVINGS

1. Mix all the ingredients together in a blender or food processor until smooth.

2. Serve cold.

You can use this chutney as a spread on toast or mixed with warm pasta as a pesto. Since cilantro starts to darken and turn brown when kept in contact with moisture, this chutney will start to lose its robust green color if kept out for too long. Though it's best to enjoy this chutney fresh, if you have any leftovers, you can keep it in the fridge for a day or two, stored in an airtight container.

Salmon with Blueberry Chutney

INGREDIENTS

2 cups blueberries
$\frac{1}{2}$ cup minced onion
$\frac{1}{2}$ teaspoon ground ginger
$\frac{1}{3}$ cup apple cider vinegar
$\frac{1}{2}$ cup brown sugar
2 tablespoons cornstarch
6 (4–5-ounce) skinless salmon fillets

1 teaspoon salt
$\frac{1}{8}$ teaspoon white pepper
1 teaspoon dried thyme leaves
$\frac{1}{4}$ cup orange juice

YIELD: 6 SERVINGS

1. In medium microwave-safe bowl, combine blueberries, onion, ginger, vinegar, and brown sugar.

2. Cover and microwave on high for 2 minutes, remove, and stir. Add cornstarch, mix well, and microwave for another 2 minutes. Remove and cool.

3. Place salmon in microwave-safe dish. Sprinkle with salt, pepper, and thyme. Add orange juice.

4. Cover and microwave on high for 8–12 minutes, rearranging salmon once, until salmon flakes. Let stand for 5 minutes, then serve with chutney.

This chutney can be made with other fruits. Substitute chopped peaches or nectarines, or chopped strawberries or pears. You can make the chutney ahead of time. Refrigerate it up to 2 days. It can be served cold with the fish, or reheat it in the microwave.

Red Chile Salsa

INGREDIENTS

3 beefsteak tomatoes
1/2 onion, peeled
4 dried guajillo chiles
1 red bell pepper
1 cup cilantro leaves
4 garlic cloves, peeled
2 tablespoons olive oil
2 limes, juiced
1 tablespoon vinegar
1 teaspoon salt

YIELD: 4-6 SERVINGS

1. Coarsely chop the tomatoes, discarding the watery seed portion, and cut the onion into large chunks.

2. Heat a comal (a type of griddle typically used in Mexican cooking) slowly to high heat. Place the dried chiles on the hot comal and toast about 30 seconds on each side until browned and fragrant.

3. Soak the toasted chiles in warm water 30 minutes or until softened.

4. Cut the stems off the chiles and use a spoon to scrape out the seeds. Cut into chunks.

5. Cut the stem off the bell pepper, remove the seeds, and cut into chunks.

6. Add all ingredients to a food processor and process a few seconds at a time until the ingredients are well combined.

Guajillos are a great choice for this salsa because they have a rich, earthy flavor but are not overpowering.

Salsa Verde

INGREDIENTS

12 tomatillos
4 Anaheim chiles
1 medium white onion
1 bunch cilantro
5 cloves garlic
1 teaspoon vegetable oil
1 tablespoon lime juice
Salt to taste
$\frac{1}{2}$ cup water, as needed

YIELD: 4-6 SERVINGS

1. Remove the husks from the tomatillos, rinse them thoroughly to remove the sticky residue, and then cut them into quarters.

2. Char the Anaheim chiles under a broiler and remove the skins, seeds, and stems.

3. Coarsely chop the onion and cilantro.

4. Add all the ingredients except the water to a food processor and mix on low speed until ingredients are combined. The mixture should not be thick. If it is too thick, add the water a little at a time, processing after each addition, until a thinner consistency is achieved. It should be about as thin as tomato sauce.

Salsa verde, or green salsa, is different from green chile sauce because it contains tomatillos, which give the salsa its signature flavor. It can be served warm as in a stew-type dish or lightly chilled or at room temperature as a condiment or topping.

Roasted Chile Salsa

INGREDIENTS

1 pound large, fresh red chiles such as Anaheim
1 red bell pepper
1 onion, cut into quarters
6 garlic cloves

1 pound ripe tomatoes
1 cup cilantro leaves
3 tablespoons vinegar
1 teaspoon salt

YIELD: 4–6 SERVINGS

1. Roast the chiles and bell pepper until the skins are blackened. Peel the skins off and remove the stems and seeds.

2. Place the onion quarters, garlic, and tomatoes onto a baking sheet and brown them under a broiler.

3. Let the tomatoes cool, cut the stem area out, and use a spoon to scoop out the majority of the seeds and liquid.

4. Place all the ingredients into a food processor and process until combined.

If fresh red chiles are not available, substitute fresh green chiles such as New Mexico or poblano chiles. The green chiles will give the salsa a more muted neutral color rather than a bright red tone, but it will still have excellent flavor.

Marinated Eggplant with Onion Tomato Salsa

INGREDIENTS

¼ cup olive oil
3 tablespoons lemon juice
½ teaspoon dried thyme leaves
½ teaspoon salt
⅛ teaspoon pepper
1 eggplant, peeled and sliced
1 onion, sliced
1 sweet red onion, sliced
2 red tomatoes, halved
1 tablespoon minced fresh mint
1 tablespoon minced cilantro leaves
3 tablespoons crumbled blue cheese

YIELD: 4-6 SERVINGS

1. In small bowl, combine oil, lemon juice, thyme, salt, pepper. Pour into 13-inch x 9-inch glass baking dish.

2. Slice eggplant into rounds; add to dish. Skewer onions and add to dish. Cover; marinate for 30–40 minutes. Prepare grill for medium-high direct heat.

3. Remove vegetables from marinade; reserve marinade. Grill vegetables, turning once, until tender, about 5–7 minutes.

4. Place eggplant on platter. Chop onions and tomatoes; mix with reserved marinade, mint, cilantro, blue cheese; spoon over eggplant.

Herbed Salsa Pork Chops

INGREDIENTS

¼ cup salt
¼ cup sugar
6 cups water
6 1-inch-thick center cut loin pork chops
2 tablespoons olive oil
⅓ cup salsa
2 tablespoons low-sodium soy sauce
¼ cup apple cider vinegar
2 tablespoons chopped fresh thyme leaves
2 tablespoons chopped flat-leaf parsley
1 tablespoon chopped fresh marjoram leaves
⅛ teaspoon white pepper

YIELD: 6 SERVINGS

1. Combine salt, sugar, and water. Add chops; cover; chill for 10–12 hours.

2. Remove chops from brine; rinse well and pat dry. Brush with olive oil. In shallow bowl, combine salsa, soy sauce, vinegar, herbs, and pepper and mix well.

3. Grill chops over medium direct heat for 10–12 minutes, turning and brushing with salsa mixture, until meat thermometer registers 155°F.

4. Pour remaining marinade into small saucepan; boil for 1 minute and pour over chops. Let stand for 1 minute, then serve.

Brines are weaker marinades used to force moisture into food. Make sure that the food you brine is natural, not enhanced. Enhanced meats are already injected with brine. Don't worry about the health effects of salt in brines. The food doesn't absorb much sodium. The salt concentrations between the brine and flesh must equalize, drawing liquid into the meat.

Real Peanut Sauce

INGREDIENTS

1 cup fresh-tasting dry-roasted peanuts,
  unsalted

2 cloves garlic, minced

2 tablespoons fish sauce (vegetarians substitute
  2½ tablespoons soy sauce)

½ teaspoon dark soy sauce

½ teaspoon tamarind paste OR 1 tablespoon
  lime juice

2 teaspoons sesame oil

2 tablespoons brown sugar

1–2 teaspoons Thai chili sauce OR $1/2$–$3/4$
teaspoon cayenne pepper, to taste

$1/4$ cup water

$1/2$ cup coconut milk

YIELD: 6+ SERVINGS

1. Place peanuts in a food processor or blender.

2. Pulse until nuts are ground to preferred consistency: coarsely ground if you prefer a chunkier sauce, or more finely ground for a smoother sauce.

3. Add all the other ingredients to the food processor or blender and blend to create a delicious peanut sauce. If you prefer a runnier sauce, add a little more water or coconut milk.

4. Serve with chicken or pork satay, on dumplings, or as a dip for fresh vegetables.

When shopping for peanuts for this recipe, look for crunchy, fresh-tasting dry-roasted nuts. Bulk peanuts are usually fine, so long as they are crisp on the outside (not soft). Also, note that this sauce tends to thicken as it sits. Just add a little more water or coconut milk to bring it back to your preferred consistency.

Nam Prik Pao Chili Sauce

INGREDIENTS

¼ cup vegetable oil such as canola
2 shallots, minced
4 cloves garlic, minced
3 tablespoons ground dry-roasted red chiles
  OR 3 tablespoons cayenne pepper
¾ teaspoon shrimp paste
2½–3 tablespoons fish sauce, to taste
2–3 tablespoons palm sugar OR brown sugar
½ teaspoon tamarind paste
3–4 tablespoons water, divided

YIELD: 1 SMALL BOTTLE OF CHILI SAUCE

1. Warm a wok or small frying pan over
   medium-high heat. Add the oil, plus the
   chopped shallots and garlic. Stir-fry until
   slightly crispy (2–3 minutes). Remove with a
   slotted spoon and place in a bowl. Remove
   wok from heat, reserving oil for later.

2. Place the other ingredients in a mini chopper
   or food processor. Add the garlic and shallots.

3. Process into a thick paste. This step can
   also be accomplished using a pestle and
   mortar, gradually adding the liquid after the
   ingredients have been pounded together.

4. Combine this mixture with the reserved oil in the wok or frying pan. Set over low heat and lightly simmer, stirring continuously.

5. Adjust the sauce in terms of consistency, adding 1–2 tablespoons water for a runnier sauce, or more oil. Season with more fish sauce or sugar to taste.

6. Pour the sauce into a jar and refrigerate. Nam prik pao will keep for a month or longer. It goes well with nearly any Thai dish, and is a must with noodles and fried rice.

Fresh Mango Sauce

INGREDIENTS

1 ripe mango
1-2 tablespoons palm sugar OR brown sugar, to
  taste
1 tablespoon fish sauce (OR 1½ tablespoons soy
  sauce if vegetarian)
1 tablespoon lime juice
2-4 tablespoons good-quality coconut milk
½ teaspoon cayenne pepper OR 1 teaspoon
  Thai chili sauce (optional)

YIELD: 6 SERVINGS

1. Hold the mango on its side and cut it into 3
   parts, being careful to slice on either side of
   the central (flat) stone.

2. You will end up with 2 rounded pieces of
   mango (either side of the fruit) and the flat,
   central slice, which contains the stone. Using
   a tablespoon, scoop out the fruit from the
   end pieces.

3. Peel off the skin around the stone and use a
   knife to cut off any remaining fruit.

4. Place all the mango fruit and sugar in a
   blender or food processor. Blend to create a
   smooth mango puree.

5. Add the remaining ingredients and blend again (add more coconut milk for a runnier sauce).

6. Taste-test the sauce, adding more sugar if too sour, or more chili sauce if you prefer it spicier. If too sweet or salty, add another squeeze of lime juice. Enjoy on dishes of your choice.

Easy Coconut Dip

INGREDIENTS

¼ cup thick coconut milk
1 clove garlic, minced
2 tablespoons fish sauce (OR 2½ tablespoons
  soy sauce if vegetarian)
1 tablespoon lime juice
1 teaspoon fresh-cut red chile, de-seeded, OR
  ½–1½ teaspoons dried chile flakes
1–3 teaspoons brown sugar, to taste
Fresh coriander for garnish

YIELD: SERVES UP TO 6 PEOPLE AS A DIP

1. Place coconut milk in a mixing bowl.

2. Add the garlic, fish sauce, lime juice, chili, and 1 teaspoon brown sugar.

3. Stir together and taste-test the dip, adding more fish sauce if not salty enough, or more lime juice if too salty or too sweet.

4. If you find the sauce is too thin, simply place in the refrigerator for 30 minutes (the coconut milk will naturally thicken with the lower temperature).

5. Add fresh cilantro as a garnish, and sprinkle over a little more fresh chile (or chile flakes) if desired. Store covered in the refrigerator for up to 6 days. Enjoy as a dipping sauce with shrimp.

For this dip, it's best to use good-quality coconut milk. If your coconut milk includes a layer of cream on the top of the can, be sure to include at least 2 tablespoons of this (plus 1 tablespoon of the coconut water), as it will give you the best coconut flavor.

Hot Sweet Thai Sauce

INGREDIENTS

2 tablespoons soy sauce
$1/2$ teaspoon cornstarch
$1/4$ cup good-quality chicken stock
1 tablespoon fish sauce
1 fresh-cut red chile OR 1–2 teaspoons Thai chili
  sauce OR $1/2$–$3/4$ teaspoon cayenne pepper, to
  taste
1–2 green onions, sliced finely
1 tablespoon freshly squeezed lime juice
2 tablespoons palm sugar OR brown sugar

YIELD: 2–4 SERVINGS

1. Measure the soy sauce into a cup. Add
   the cornstarch and stir until it dissolves
   completely.

2. This will be the thickener for your sauce. Set
   this mixture aside, near the stove.

3. Get out a saucepan and pour in the chicken
   stock.

4. Add the fish sauce, chile, onion, lime juice,
   and sugar to the saucepan. Bring to a boil.

5. Reduce heat to medium and add the
   reserved soy sauce/cornstarch mixture.

6. Stir occasionally until sauce thickens (1–2 minutes). Remove from heat. Serve warm with Thai grilled fish or meats, or with fresh spring rolls or dumplings.

Chile and Garlic Sauce

INGREDIENTS

4–5 cloves garlic
$1/4$ teaspoon chile flakes
2 tablespoons soy sauce
1 tablespoon fish sauce
2 tablespoons lime juice
2 tablespoons Thai sweet chili sauce
2 tablespoons brown sugar
$1/2$ tablespoon oyster sauce
3 tablespoons coconut milk

YIELD: MAKES APPROXIMATELY $1/2$ CUP SAUCE

1. Mince the garlic by processing it in a mini chopper, or by using a garlic press. You can also chop it up very finely with a knife. Set aside.

2. Combine all other ingredients together in a bowl, stirring to dissolve the sugar. Set aside.

3. Heat 1–2 tablespoons oil in a wok or small frying pan over medium-high heat.

4. Add the minced garlic and stir-fry until fragrant, but not so long that it turns brown or bitter (1 minute).

5. Reduce heat to low. Add the previously combined ingredients, stirring well.

6. Taste-test the sauce for sweetness and spice, adding more sugar if too sour, or more chile if you prefer it spicier. If not salty or flavorful enough, add more fish sauce. If too sweet or too salty, add more fresh lime juice.

7. Serve the sauce with your choice of grilled meats, fish, or seafood.

Asparagus Tempura with Chive Mayo Dipping Sauce

INGREDIENTS

1½ pounds fresh asparagus
1 egg
½–1 cup ice water
1 tablespoon sake (Japanese rice wine)
¾ cup all-purpose flour
¼ cup finely ground cornmeal

Oil (for frying)
1/2 cup mayonnaise
1/4 cup plain yogurt
3 tablespoons white wine
1/4 cup minced fresh chives
1 tablespoon fresh lemon juice
1 tablespoon minced fresh thyme
1 teaspoon fresh dill weed
Salt and pepper

YIELD: 4 SERVINGS

1. Wash and dry the asparagus and cut off the thick ends.

2. Beat the egg, then add the ice water, beating until the mixture is light. Add the sake.

3. Mix the flours together and sift them into the egg mixture. Stir until blended.

4. Heat the oil to 340°F. Dip the asparagus, a few stalks at a time, into the batter and fry 3–5 minutes, until golden brown. Drain on paper towels.

5. Combine the mayonnaise, yogurt, wine, chives, thyme, lemon juice, and dill. Add salt and pepper to taste. Serve asparagus with the dipping sauce.

Salmon with
Sweet Pepper Sauce

INGREDIENTS

Sweet Pepper Sauce:
2 red bell peppers, roasted, peeled, and seeded
  (available by the jar in supermarkets)
2 garlic cloves, finely chopped
3 tablespoons freshly squeezed lemon juice
1/2 cup low-fat mayonnaise
1 pinch cayenne pepper
1 teaspoon chile powder
1 teaspoon honey

2 tablespoons olive oil
2 tablespoons freshly ground black pepper
4 (6-ounce) salmon steaks

YIELD: 4 SERVINGS

1. Preheat the broiler.

2. Make the Sweet Pepper Sauce: In a food
   processor or blender, combine the bell
   peppers, garlic, lemon juice, mayonnaise,
   cayenne pepper, chile powder, and honey.

3. Mix on high speed for 30 seconds or with a
   hand blender for 1–2 minutes until blended
   well. Set aside.

4. Pour the oil onto a plate. Place the black pepper on another plate. Dip the salmon in the oil, then press it into the pepper.

5. Broil the salmon, turning once after 4 minutes for medium-rare. When the salmon sweats, the fish is done. Serve with Sweet Pepper Sauce for dipping on the side, approximately 2 tablespoons per serving.

Spaghetti with Tomato Turkey Sauce

INGREDIENTS

1 tablespoon olive oil
1 pound ground turkey
1 onion, chopped
4 cloves garlic, minced
1 (6-ounce) can tomato paste
2 (14-ounce) cans diced tomatoes, undrained
1 cup tomato juice
2 teaspoons sugar

$\frac{1}{2}$ teaspoon salt

$1\frac{1}{2}$ teaspoons dried basil leaves

$\frac{1}{2}$ teaspoon dried oregano leaves

$\frac{1}{4}$ teaspoon pepper

1 (16-ounce) package spaghetti

$\frac{1}{2}$ cup grated Romano cheese

YIELD: 6 SERVINGS

1. In large saucepan, heat olive oil; add turkey, onion, and garlic. Cook and stir until turkey is tender; drain.

2. Add tomato paste; let brown in spots, then add tomatoes, juice, and remaining ingredients except spaghetti and cheese.

3. Let the sauce simmer, stirring occasionally. Bring a large pot of salted water to a boil. Cook pasta until al dente.

4. Drain pasta. Spoon sauce over pasta. Sprinkle with cheese; serve.

Fresh Tomato-Basil Sauce

INGREDIENTS

5 pounds ripe plum tomatoes OR 3 (28-ounce)
  cans crushed plum tomatoes
½ cup extra-virgin olive oil
½ cup diced onion
3 garlic cloves, minced
1½ cups dry red wine
Salt and red pepper flakes, to taste
5 large sprigs basil

YIELD: 10 CUPS

1. Core and puree the tomatoes.

2. In a deep heavy pot, heat the olive oil.
   Add the onion, and sauté until soft. Add
   the garlic, and sauté until soft. Add the
   tomatoes; stir to blend.

3. Add the wine, salt, red pepper flakes, and
   basil, stirring well. Bring to a boil, reduce the
   heat, and simmer for 25 minutes.

4. The sauce is ready to be used. It can also be
   refrigerated for up to a week, or frozen for up
   to 3 months.

Fresh basil is essential to Italian cooking, but it can be very expensive to buy it in stores. This herb is easy to grow in the garden in summer, and on a sunny windowsill in winter. Pick the leaves regularly and don't let the plants develop flowers, for all the energy will then go into developing seeds. You can freeze basil leaves whole for longer storage.

Scampi with Tomato Sauce

INGREDIENTS

2 pounds scampi or large shrimp
1 onion, diced
1 garlic clove, minced
4–5 tablespoons olive oil
2 bay leaves
1 small pepperocini (or red chile), finely
  chopped
1 (28-ounce) can plum tomatoes
Salt, to taste
3/4 cup dry white wine
1 tablespoon freshly chopped Italian parsley

YIELD: 3–4 SERVINGS

1. Peel and devein the shrimp.

2. Cut the scampi in half lengthwise, and wash
   thoroughly under cold running water.

3. In a large pan, sauté the onion and garlic in
   oil. Add the bay leaves and pepperocini.

4. Pour in the plum tomatoes with their juices.
   Cover and simmer over medium-low heat for
   10–15 minutes.

5. Add the scampi and salt to taste. Pour in the
   wine, and simmer for 4 minutes covered.

6. Arrange the scampi on a plate; pour over some of the cooking juices, and garnish with the parsley.

Look for San Marzano canned tomatoes from Italy. This variety of plum tomato is considered the best choice for tomato sauce. Grown in the San Marzano area near Naples, this tomato has thicker flesh and fewer seeds and tastes sweeter and less acidic.

Meatballs in Tomato Sauce

INGREDIENTS

1 cup finely chopped onion
6 garlic cloves, minced, divided
2 tablespoons unsalted butter, divided
2 tablespoons chopped parsley
1 teaspoon dried oregano
2 tablespoons grated Romano cheese
1 (6-ounce) can no-salt-added tomato paste, divided
$\frac{1}{4}$ teaspoon pepper
1 cup soft fresh bread crumbs
1$\frac{1}{4}$ pounds 80 percent lean ground beef
2 (14.5-ounce) cans no-salt-added diced tomatoes

3 tablespoons vodka
½ cup light cream
¼ cup chopped parsley
½ teaspoon crushed red pepper flakes

YIELD: 6 SERVINGS

1. Cook minced onion and 2 cloves garlic in half the butter until tender.

2. Place in bowl with parsley, oregano, cheese, 1 tablespoon tomato paste, pepper, and bread crumbs.

3. Add ground beef; form into 24 meatballs. Brown in same saucepan in remaining butter; remove and set aside.

4. In same saucepan, cook 4 cloves garlic. Add remaining tomato paste, tomatoes, vodka, cream, parsley, and red pepper flakes; simmer 5 minutes. Add meatballs; simmer 40 minutes. Serve over hot cooked pasta.

> To form meatballs quickly and evenly, use a small ice cream scoop. A 2-tablespoon scoop is just about the right size. Dip into the ground beef mixture and form a ball; smooth out the edges with your hands. This method will make very tender meatballs because they aren't overworked.

Risotto with Meat Sauce

INGREDIENTS

1 cup dried porcini mushrooms (about 1 ounce)
6 tablespoons ($^3/_4$ stick) butter
2 cups arborio rice
2 tablespoons heavy cream
1 cup freshly grated Parmigiano Reggiano

Ragu:
$^1/_4$ cup olive oil
1 white onion, thinly sliced
$^1/_2$ pound sweet Italian sausage, casings removed
2 cups chopped fresh or canned plum tomatoes
$^1/_2$ cup water
Salt, to taste

YIELD: 8 SERVINGS

1. Soak the porcini mushrooms in 4 cups of cold water until soft, about 30 minutes. Drain the mushrooms in a colander over a bowl.

2. Dice the mushrooms; set aside. Strain the porcini liquid several times to remove any sand. Pour it into a saucepan, and bring it to barely a boil. Keep warm over very low heat.

3. In a large skillet, heat the oil, add the onion, and sauté until almost caramelized.

4. Add the sausages, breaking apart and

browning the meat. Stir in the tomatoes, $1/2$ cup water, and salt, mixing well.

5. Simmer until thickened, about 15 minutes. Transfer to a food processor and blend until smooth. Set aside in a bowl.

6. Melt butter over medium heat. Add rice; cook for 1–2 minutes, stirring. When rice begins to crackle, reduce heat to medium-low and add $1/4$ cup of reserved porcini liquid. Cook, stirring, until absorbed. Add $1/4$ cup of ragu and cook, stirring, until absorbed. Add remaining porcini liquid and sauce to rice alternately, $1/4$ cup at a time, letting the rice absorb all liquid before adding more.

7. Stir in cream. Remove from heat; stir in cheese.

Veal with Pizza Sauce

INGREDIENTS

1/4 cup olive oil

3 garlic cloves, finely chopped

4 cups coarsely chopped fresh plum tomatoes (canned is fine)—about 8 medium-size tomatoes

2 teaspoons salt

1 1/2 tablespoons chopped fresh oregano OR 1 tablespoon dried

1/4 cup chopped fresh basil

2 tablespoons butter

1 pound veal cutlets

1/2 cup flour, seasoned with salt and white pepper

1/4 cup chopped fresh parsley

YIELD: 4 SERVINGS

1. In a large skillet, heat the oil and sauté the garlic until soft. Add the tomatoes, salt, and oregano.

2. Simmer over low heat for about 15 minutes, or until slightly thickened. Remove from the heat; stir in the basil, and set aside.

3. Pat the veal dry with a paper towel. With a meat mallet, pound all the veal cutlets between sheets of plastic wrap or waxed paper.

4. Season the veal cutlets on both sides with salt and pepper. Right before cooking, dredge the veal cutlets in the seasoned flour. Shake off any excess flour.

5. In a large skillet, melt the butter, add the veal, and sauté until lightly brown on both sides, about 2 minutes. Add the tomato sauce and simmer for about 5 minutes. Stir in the parsley.

Calabrese Meat Sauce

INGREDIENTS

2 tablespoons olive oil
2 garlic cloves, chopped
1 medium-size onion, coarsely chopped
1 celery rib, coarsely chopped
1 large carrot, coarsely chopped
1 pound beef round or chuck steak, cut into 1/2-inch cubes
1 pound pork tenderloin, cut into 1/2-inch cubes

½ cup red dry wine
3 (28-ounce) cans plum tomatoes
1 bay leaf
1 tablespoon salt

YIELD: 8 CUPS

1. In a large saucepan, heat the oil. Add the garlic, and sauté until soft. Add the onion, celery, and carrot; sauté for 5–7 minutes, or until soft.

2. Using a slotted spoon, remove the vegetables from the pan. Set aside.

3. Pat the meat dry with paper towels; add to the pan in which the vegetables were cooked, and brown it well.

4. Add the wine, and simmer for 5 minutes.

5. Add the tomatoes, bay leaf, and salt. Return the vegetables to the pan.

6. Simmer the ragu, covered, over low heat until the meat is tender, about 45 minutes.

7. Remove and discard the bay leaf. Use immediately, or freeze for up to 3 months.

8. Serve over chunky types of pasta, such as penne, or over slices of polenta.

Grilled Tomato and Shrimp Sauce

INGREDIENTS

2 pounds fresh tomatoes, halved
1 teaspoon salt, divided
1 onion, sliced
4 cloves garlic, peeled
2 tablespoons olive oil
1 tablespoon lemon juice
1 teaspoon paprika
$\frac{1}{2}$ teaspoon dried oregano leaves
$\frac{1}{2}$ teaspoon dried basil leaves
$\frac{1}{8}$ teaspoon cayenne pepper
1 pound medium raw shrimp, shelled
1 (12-ounce) package ridged spaghetti pasta
$\frac{1}{3}$ cup grated Romano cheese

YIELD: 6 SERVINGS

1. Bring pot of salted water to a boil. Sprinkle tomatoes with $\frac{1}{2}$ teaspoon salt. Skewer onion slices and garlic cloves.

2. Mix olive oil, lemon juice, paprika, $\frac{1}{2}$ teaspoon salt, oregano, basil, and cayenne pepper. Toss with shrimp; let stand for 15 minutes.

3. Grill tomatoes, onion, and garlic. Remove tomato skins, chop, and add flesh to a large bowl. Chop onion and garlic.

4. Grill shrimp for 4–6 minutes; add to bowl. Cook pasta, drain and add to bowl; toss. Sprinkle with cheese and serve.

Butter and Cream Sauce

INGREDIENTS

3 tablespoons butter
1 cup heavy cream
Pinch freshly ground nutmeg
Salt and freshly ground black pepper
½–1 cup grated Parmigiano Reggiano cheese
I pound cooked pasta (fettuccine is
   recommended)

YIELD: 3–4 SERVINGS

1. In a large skillet over medium-high heat, combine the butter and cream. Bring to a boil, stirring frequently until the cream has reduced almost by half.

2. Add the nutmeg, salt, and a generous amount of black pepper. Remove from the heat.

3. Add the freshly grated cheese to the skillet, then add the cooked pasta, tossing well to coat with sauce. Season to taste with more salt and pepper.

The type of butter you use can affect the creaminess of simple sauces. Unsalted butter makes the creamiest sauces, and using this product lets you control the amount of sodium you put in your food. Salted butter is less expensive, and unless you are serving real gourmets, the sauce made from it will still be creamy and delicious. The choice is yours!

Basic White Sauce

INGREDIENTS

2 tablespoons low-fat margarine
2 shallots, peeled and minced
2 tablespoons all-purpose flour
1 cup warm low-fat milk
$\frac{1}{2}$ teaspoon salt
$\frac{1}{4}$ teaspoon Worcestershire sauce
$\frac{1}{2}$ teaspoon ground white pepper
Optional: $\frac{1}{8}$ teaspoon ground nutmeg; 1
   teaspoon chopped chives; 1 teaspoon
   sweet paprika; 1 hard-boiled egg, chopped;
   1 teaspoon curry powder; or 1 teaspoon
   prepared Dijon-style mustard

YIELD: 1 CUP (4 $\frac{1}{4}$-CUP SERVINGS)

1. Heat margarine in a saucepan over medium
   heat. Stir in minced shallot and cook until
   softened.

2. Whisk in flour and cook, stirring until well
   blended with the margarine, about 3 minutes.

3. Stir in warm milk, adding it slowly and
   making sure it blends, or you will have lumps.

4. Mix in salt, Worcestershire sauce, and pepper.
   Reduce heat to low, and stir until very
   smooth and creamy. Add any of the optional
   ingredients you desire; serve.

To turn this into a brown sauce, add $\frac{1}{2}$ cup chopped mushrooms when you are sautéing the shallots in the melted margarine. Substitute warm beef broth for the warm milk. Follow the recipe as directed omitting the nutmeg. Serve with roast beef or steak, or add to stew. You may also flavor a brown sauce with $\frac{1}{4}$ cup red wine.

Fish in Saffron Cream Sauce

INGREDIENTS

1½ pounds sole or flounder fillets
3-4 tablespoons fresh lemon juice, divided
Salt and freshly ground pepper
1 tablespoon butter
2 shallots, peeled and minced
1¼ cups fish stock
½ cup heavy cream
⅛-¼ teaspoon crumbled saffron threads
  (available in any specialty food store)
2-3 tablespoons water

YIELD: 4 SERVINGS

1. Drizzle the fillets with 2 tablespoons of the lemon juice; season with salt and pepper.

2. In a large skillet, melt the butter over medium heat. Sauté shallots until translucent.

3. Add the stock to the pan, bring to a boil, and reduce to a simmer.

4. Place half of the fish fillets in the skillet containing the simmering broth. Cover and cook for 2-3 minutes.

5. Transfer the fish to a warmed serving dish; cover to keep warm.

6. Sauté the rest of fish in the same way, and keep warm.

7. Stir the cream into the skillet. Dissolve the saffron in water; add to the skillet. Let the sauce cook for 30 minutes, or until very creamy.

8. Season with salt, pepper, and the remaining lemon juice. Lay the fish in the hot sauce to heat through before serving.

Red Pepper Cream Sauce

INGREDIENTS

Olive oil to coat
4 red bell peppers
$1/4$ cup ($1/2$ stick) butter
2 garlic cloves, minced
1 cup heavy cream or half-and-half
1 teaspoon grated nutmeg
$1^1/2$ teaspoons salt
$1/4$ teaspoon freshly grated black pepper
$1/4$ cup minced fresh basil

YIELD: 3 CUPS

1. Coat the peppers with olive oil and place them on a lightly greased baking sheet. Broil, turning occasionally, until blackened all over, about 15 minutes.

2. Place the peppers in a large paper bag, close the bag tightly, and set aside for 25 minutes to let them steam.

3. Peel the roasted peppers. The charred skin will come off easily. Remove the seeds and cores.

4. Place the peppers in a food processor, and puree until smooth. Set aside.

5. In a large frying pan, heat the butter, and sauté the garlic over medium heat until soft. Add the pepper puree and mix well. Reduce the heat and gradually stir in the heavy cream. Add the nutmeg, salt, and pepper; cook, stirring, for 5 minutes. Remove from the heat, and stir in the basil.

6. Serve over pasta or as a dipping sauce for lobster.

Gorgonzola-Mushroom Sauce

INGREDIENTS

2 tablespoons olive oil
2$\frac{1}{2}$ cups sliced button mushrooms
1 garlic clove, crushed
1$\frac{1}{4}$ cups light cream
6 ounces Gorgonzola cheese, rind removed, crumbled
Salt and ground black pepper
1 pound pasta, cooked
1 tablespoon chopped fresh parsley
$\frac{1}{2}$ cup chopped walnuts

YIELD: 2 SERVINGS

1. Heat the olive oil in a pan over medium heat, and sauté the mushrooms for 5 minutes.

2. Add the garlic and cook for 1–2 more minutes. Stir in the cream, bring to a boil, and cook for 1 minute. Stir in the Gorgonzola.

3. Reheat gently to melt the cheese; do not boil. Season with salt and pepper. Add the sauce to cooked pasta.

4. Garnish with chopped parsley and walnuts.

Tuna with Mushroom Sauce

INGREDIENTS

4 tuna steaks, 6 ounces each
Salt and cayenne pepper
¼ cup (½ stick) unsalted butter

Mushroom Sauce:
1 shallot, finely chopped
6 ounces assorted mushrooms, trimmed
  and sliced

1 cup chicken or vegetable stock (low-sodium)

2 teaspoons cornstarch

$1/2$ teaspoon prepared mustard

$1/4$ cup heavy cream

3 tablespoons chopped fresh tarragon

1 teaspoon white wine vinegar

YIELD: 4 SERVINGS

1. Season the tuna steaks with salt and cayenne pepper.

2. In a large frying pan, cook the tuna in the melted butter for 5 minutes, turning once.

3. Transfer the cooked tuna to a plate; cover and keep warm.

4. In the same frying pan in which you cooked the tuna steaks, heat the remaining butter and fry the shallot until soft.

5. Add the mushrooms; cook until their juices begin to flow. Add the stock and simmer for 2–3 minutes.

6. Combine the cornstarch and mustard; blend with 1 tablespoon of water. Stir into the mushroom mixture. Bring to a simmer, stirring to thicken.

7. Add the cream, tarragon, and vinegar. Season to taste; simmer for 3 more minutes. Spoon sauce over each tuna steak.

CREAM SAUCES

Pork with Smoked Cheese Sauce

8 small to medium-size pork chops
2 tablespoons butter, divided
1 tablespoon extra-virgin olive oil
Salt and black pepper
2 garlic cloves, crushed
2½ cups button mushrooms, sliced
1 cup frozen peas
¼ cup brandy
1 cup heavy cream
5 ounces smoked sheep's-milk cheese
  (Manchego or Idiazabal, available in most
  supermarkets), diced
Italian flat-leaf parsley, for garnish

YIELD: 4 SERVINGS

1. Melt half the butter with the oil in a large
    heavy-bottomed frying pan.

2. Season the chops with salt and pepper, and
    brown them on each side in batches over
    medium-high heat.

3. Reduce the heat, and cook for about 7
    minutes on each side until just done. The
    cooked chops should feel firm to the touch,
    with a very light springiness.

4. Remove the chops to a serving dish; keep hot. Add the remaining butter to the pan. Stir-fry the garlic and mushrooms for 3 minutes.

5. Add the peas and brandy; cook until the pan juices have been absorbed. Using a slotted spoon, place mushrooms and peas on top of chops.

6. Pour the heavy cream into the frying pan, and mix well. Stir in the diced cheese.

7. Over medium-low heat, stir constantly until the cheese has melted.

8. Season with pepper only. The cheese adds enough salt to flavor the sauce. Pour sauce over chops, garnishing with parsley.

BOOKS

Gayler, Paul. *The Sauce Book,*
Kyle Books, 2009.
A guide to making over 300 sauces with no fuss.

Lee, Sonja. *Sauce,* Gold Street Press, 2008.
The authoritative book on sauces, dressings, dips, and
spreads.

Peterson, James. *Sauces: Classical and
Contemporary Sauce Making,* Wiley, 2008.
A comprehensive look at all things sauce—with over
400 recipes.

WEB SITES

AllRecipes.com
http://allrecipes.com
This site features reader-submitted recipes that
are rated by members. Recipes can be filtered by
ingredient using the search feature.

Bon Appétit

www.bonappetit.com

Always features a variety of dishes with a unique spin on everyday ingredients.

Ciao Italia

www.ciaoitalia.com

A focus on all things Italian.

Cooks.com

www.cooks.com

Any and all recipes, vegetable and otherwise, along with many tips, nutrition facts, and forums.

Epicurious

www.epicurious.com

Find virtually any sauce recipe here, with helpful slideshows and commentary.

Food Network

www.foodnetwork.com

Like the TV shows, the Web site for the food network is packed with information, from recipes to techniques.

Giada De Laurentiis

www.giadadelaurentiis.com

The acclaimed Italian chef, TV personality, and author.

The Italian Chef

www.italianchef.com

Homemade sauce recipes; blog updated regularly.

Whole Foods Market

www.wholefoodsmarket.com/recipes

Search for delicious sauce recipes and new inspirations for using your favorite ingredients

APPROXIMATE U.S.–METRIC EQUIVALENTS

LIQUID INGREDIENTS

U.S. Measures	Metric	U.S. Measures	Metric
$1/4$ tsp.	1.23 ml	2 Tbsp.	29.57 ml
$1/2$ tsp.	2.36 ml	3 Tbsp.	44.36 ml
$3/4$ tsp.	3.70 ml	$1/4$ cup	59.15 ml
1 tsp.	4.93 ml	$1/2$ cup	118.30 ml
$1^{1/4}$ tsp.	6.16 ml	1 cup	236.59 ml
$1^{1/2}$ tsp.	7.39 ml	2 cups or 1 pt.	473.18 ml
$1^{3/4}$ tsp.	8.63 ml	3 cups	709.77 ml
2 tsp.	9.86 ml	4 cups or 1 qt.	946.36 ml
1 Tbsp.	14.79 ml	4 qts. or 1 gal.	3.79 l

DRY INGREDIENTS

U.S. Measures	Metric	U.S. Measures	Metric
$1/16$ oz.	2 (1.8) g	$2^{4/5}$ oz.	80 g
$1/8$ oz.	$3^{1/2}$ (3.5) g	3 oz.	85 (84.9) g
$1/4$ oz.	7 (7.1) g	$3^{1/2}$ oz.	100 g
$1/2$ oz.	15 (14.2) g	4 oz.	115 (113.2) g
$3/4$ oz.	21 (21.3) g	$4^{1/2}$ oz.	125 g
$7/8$ oz.	25 g	$5^{1/4}$ oz.	150 g
1 oz.	30 (28.3) g	$8^{7/8}$ oz.	250 g
$1^{3/4}$ oz.	50 g	16 oz. or 1 lb.	454 g
2 oz.	60 (56.6) g	$17^{3/5}$ oz. or 1 livre	500 g

Broil: To cook food close to the heat source, quickly.

Chop: To cut food into small pieces, using a chef's knife or a food processor.

Comal: A type of griddle typically used in Mexican cooking.

Dice: To cut food into small, even portions, usually about $1/4$ inch square.

Direct grilling: To cook food directly over a heat source, whether a burner, coals, or burning wood.

Dredge: To cover food in flour.

Grill: To cook over coals or charcoal, or over high heat.

Indirect grilling: To cook food over an area on the grill where there are no coals, usually over a drip pan.

Marinate: To allow meats or vegetables to stand in a mixture of an acid and oil, to add flavor and tenderize.

Sauté: To cook food briefly in oil over medium-high heat, while stirring it so it cooks evenly.

Seasoning: To add herbs, spices, citrus juices and zest, and peppers to food to increase flavor.

Slow cooker: An appliance that cooks food by surrounding it with low, steady heat.

Stir-fry: To quickly cook food by manipulating it with a spoon or spatula, in a wok or pan, over high heat.

Toss: To combine food using two spoons or a spoon and a fork until mixed well.

Wok: A round-bottomed pan, typically used for stir-frying, popular in China ●